Thierry Le Goues/Peter Lindbergh/Tiziano Magni/Craig McDean/Steven Meisel/Helmut Newton/Cindy Palmano/Platon/Andre Rau

Blaise Reutersward/Bettina Rheims/Terry Richardson/Francois Rotger/Paolo Roversi/Franco Rubartelli/Luis Sanchis/J.C. Sauer

Lothar Schmid/Nina Schultz/Laura Sciacovelli/Nigel Scott/Jeanloup Sieff/Christoph Sillem/Mario Sorrenti/Bert Stern/Steen Sundland

Juergen Teller/Michael Thompson/Max Vadukul/Javier Vallhonrat/Ellen Von Unwerth/Albert Watson/Jan Welters/Michael Wooley

Yves Saint Laurent - Forty Years of Creation 1958-1998

Edited by Beatrice Dupire & Hady Sy Text & Interviews: by Marie-Jose Lepicard Publishers: International Festival of Fashion Photography
Distributed by Distributed Art Publishers Editorial Consultant: Beatrice Dupire Creative Director: Hady Sy Art Direction: Douglas Lloyd, Lloyd + co)

Fashion and photography are contemporaries.

It is normal that they should have met Photography knows diverse fortunes, it has accompanied life and death, joy and grief, peace and war, sport and leisure. It has surpassed the instant. It is a witness. Photography is also a work of art when created by an artist, and of artists it has not been lacking throughout its history. As reflections of an era, fashion resembles photography and can, at times become a work of art. A confrontation between the two was inevitable and that the best photographers should be interested in fashion.

Today in New York, on the occasion of the International Festival of Fashion Photography, famous professionals have a rendezvous with unknowns. To the latter, we have suggested that they work with clothes often photographed in the past to express the emotion these clothes inspire today. It is the shock between generations and cultures which makes this exhibition interesting. It is certain that the artist's eye shows the world what to see. As Jean Cocteau said, "a painter always paints his own portrait." It is these self portraits we hope to discover, adding to those which exist of the past forty years thanks to the body of work by Yves Saint Laurent, which form this wonderful chain where the subject and the object blend because each one is a work of art.

La mode et la photographie sont contemporaines. Il est normal qu'elles se soient rencontrées. La photographie a connu des fortunes diverses elle a accompagné la vie et la mort, le bonheur et le malheur, la paix et la guerre, le sport et l'oisiveté. Elle a surpris l'instant. Elle est témoin. Elle est aussi oeuvre d'art lorsqu'elle est créée par un artiste. Et des artistes elle n'en a pas manqué depuis le début jusqu'à nos jours. Témoin de son temps, la mode lui ressemble et peut, parfois devenir oeuvre d'art. La confrontation des deux était inévitable et les meilleurs des photographes devaient s'intéresser à la mode.

Aujourd'hui à New York à l'occasion du Festival International de la photographie de mode des professionnels célèbres ont rendez-vous avec des inconnus. A ces derniers nous avons suggéré de travailler autour de vêtements souvent photographiés par le passé, et de traduire leur émotion. C'est ce choc des générations et des cultures qui fera l'intérêt de cette exposition. Il est certain que les artistes font voir le monde à travers leur regard. On sait que rien n'est moins objectif qu'un objectif et que, selon le mot de Jean Cocteau "un peintre fait toujours son propre portrait." C'est bien ces autoportraits que nous espérons découvrir et qui, ajoutés à ceux qui depuis quarante ans existent grâce à l'oeuvre d'Yves Saint Laurent vont former cette merveilleuse chaîne où le sujet et l'objet se mélangent puisqu'ils sont chacun oeuvre d'art.

Pierre Bergé/General Director, Yves Saint Laurent

Fourteen years after Diana Vreeland's tribute to Yves Saint Laurent at the Costume Institute of the Metropolitan Museum of Art, we are honored to present in New York, Yves Saint Laurent - Forty Years of Creation under the auspices of the French Ministry of Culture.

Without nostalgia, this exhibition expresses with tenderness, with violence, the emotion which the creations of Yves Saint Laurent continue to inspire in his friends, his admirers, and fashion professionals. Those who are not "in the know" discover with astonishment and pleasure that the "new" is not what they believed it to be.

In fact, the Saint Laurent style continues to influence everyday fashion, in that the idea of extremely simple elegance, which he defines as "pants, pullover, raincoat," can be seen in the style of women in every capital of the world. It is the style of a woman who has the Saint Laurent spirit even if she does not always wear his clothes and is sometimes unaware of the style she represents.

Some collections, some of his Haute Couture clothes remain vital, in that they exist before and after their creation. They are now part of our fashion heritage, reinterpreted regularly by other designers: the African collection, pantsuits, "smokings", transparencies...

His clothes have inspired timeless photographs by the greatest photographers: Richard Avedon, William Klein, Helmut Newton, Irving Penn, Jeanloup Sieff.

Sometimes a fashion photograph carries within it a secret scar: that of time, that of a dated garment. This will not be seen in this exhibition. What provocation to subject these clothes which are already history to the fresh and irreverent eye of a new generation of photographers! Everything has changed, but the clothes themselves still speak for their creator, rebellious and sublime.

It is this Yves Saint Laurent, through passion and anguish, through doubt and achievement, through isolation and fame, continues to touch us. His work and the spirit of his couture house proves he remains a man of emotions and longings.

Quatorze ans après l'hommage de Diana Vreeland à Yves Saint Laurent au Metropolitan Museum of Art, nous sommes honorés de présenter à New York sous le Haut-Patronage du Ministère français de la Culture l'exposition Yves Saint Laurent-Quarante Ans de Création.

Libre de tout esprit de rétrospective, cette exposition exprime avec tendresse, avec violence, l'émotion que continuent de susciter les créations d'Yves Saint Laurent chez ses amis, ses admirateurs, chez les professionnels de la mode et ceux qui ne font pas partie du sérail et découvrent avec étonnement que la nouveauté n'est pas celle qu'ils croyaient.

En effet, l'allure Saint Laurent continue d'influencer le mode de la rue, tant sa notion d'élégance simplissime, telle qui'l'a définie "pantalon, pull, imperméable" marque l'allure de la femme dans toutes les capitales du monde cette allure absolue d'une femme à l'esprit Saint Laurent qui ne porte pas toujours ses vêtements et ignore parfois ce qu'elle représente.

Certaines de ses collections, certains de ses vêtements de Haute Couture demeurent essentiels, en ce sens qu'il existe un avant et un après. Ils font désormais partie d'une sorte de patrimoine de mode, reinterprété régulièrement par nombre de créateurs: collections africaines, costumes masculins, smokings, transparences...

Ces créations ont inspiré aux plus grands photographes: Richard Avedon, William Klein, Helmut Newton, Irving Penn, Jeanloup Sieff, des images intemporelles.

Parfois une photographie de mode porte en elle-même sa propre cicatrice celle du temps, celle d'un vêtement daté.

Il n'en est rien dans cette exposition. Quelle insolence que de prêter ces vêtements évocateurs de quarante ans de création aux regards frais et turbulents d'une nouvelle génération de photographes! Visages, attitudes différents, histoires parallèles, les vêtements sont restés fidèles à la volonté de leur auteur: rebelles et sublimes.

C'est en cela qu'Yves Saint Laurent, au delà de la passion et de l'angoisse, du doute et de la durée, de l'isolement et du succès, continue de nous toucher à travers ses créations et l'esprit de sa maison de couture. Il demeure un homme d'émotions et de désirs.

Beatrice Dupire/Vice President of the Association for the Promotion of Photography
Hady Sy/President of the Association for the Promotion of Photography

It is rare for a journalist to follow the career of a great couturier from his very beginning, and I have had the good fortune to have seen all the collections by Yves Saint Laurent over the past forty years. All...the first one at Dior where before my eyes two American fashion editors sobbed in each other's arms: "It's Joan of Arc! France is saved..."

All the trapeze dresses, the first collection at the rue Spontini, the trousers, the mini skirts, the crepe de chine blouses with ruffled Edwardian collars, Jane in a leopard sarong, the girls of the occupation who infuriated the journalists who were older than I, the bush jackets and the odalisks, the "comme il faut" dresses for family lunches and the pantsuits for directors' meetings.

And the references: Cocteau, Mondrian, Matisse, Goya, Apollinaire...the bustiers by Lalanne, the brides like black virgins, like foolish virgins, and the bride wrapped in a cocoon of crocheted wool like a butterfly about to take off.

At the 1986 exhibition in the Museum of Decorative Arts, from room to room I saw once again all the dresses I had written down from season to season: a color photo or a full page? Certainly a cover...images dissolving into each other, images frozen in time... I had tears in my eyes as if it were my own life.

Even today, when I open my closet filled with often anonymous clothes, I see that my personal choices have been made under the lighting of Saint Laurent's sun.

This man who acknowledges his nervous breakdowns, his anguish, who goes out so rarely, has known how to accompany us in our daily lives with realism, humor, and exactitude. How was it that he could sense the change in everyday life? Surely as a means of distracting his sadness, of wearing away the hours...in the words of the poet Paul Eluard: "With forehead pressed against the window pane like those who watch in sorrow."

Il est rare pour une journaliste de suivre la carrière d'un grand couturier depuis son début - et j'ai eu la chance de voir toutes les collections d'Yves Saint Laurent pendant quarante ans. Toutes...la première chez Dior, où devant moi deux rédactrices américaines pleurèrent dans les bras l'une de l'autre: "It's Joan of Arc! France is saved!"

Toutes: les robes trapèze, la première collection de la rue Spontini, les pantalons, les minijupes, les blouses de crêpe de chine à col édouardien portées avec des tweeds couleur de landes,les princesses russes, Jane en pagne de panthère, les petites femmes des années de guerre qui indignèrent si fort les journalistes plus agés que moi, les sahariennes et les odalisques, les robes sages pour déjeuners de famille et les tailleurs pantalons pour conseils d'administration...et les citations: Cocteau, Mondrian, Matisse, Goya, Apollina re...les bustiers de Lalanne: les mariées comme des vierges noires, comme des vierges folles, et cette mariée enfermée dans un cocon de laine mèche, comme un papillon qui va s'envoler.

A l'exposition de 1986 au Musée des Arts Décoratifs, de salle en salle, je revoyais toutes ces robes que j'avais notées de saison en saison: une pleine page? Une photo couleur? La couverture sûrement...des fondus enchaînés, une image arrêtée... et j'avais les larmes aux yeux comme si c'était ma vie à moi, de salle en salle...

Aujourd'hui encore, quand j'ouvre mon armoire remplie de vêtements souvent anonymes, je vois que mes choix personnels se sont faits sous le soleil de Saint Laurent.

Cet homme qui avoue ses dépressions nerveuses ses angoisses, qui sort si peu, a su pourtant accompagner nos vies quotidiennes avec réalisme, humour, exactitude. Comment a-t-il fait pour voir "la rue"? Sans doute justement en distrayant sa tristesse, en usant ses heures, comme l'a écrit Paul Eluard: "Le front aux vitres comme font les veilleurs de chagrin...".

Marie-José Lepicard/Journalist

Catherine Trautmann/French Minister of Culture

Without doubt, it is the image of Saint Laurent which most characterizes the idea of change within continuity. After forty years of creativity, he remains the most brilliant ambassador of French fashion in the world.

C'est certainement la figure d'Yves Saint Laurent qui caractérise le plus l'idée d'une forme de nouveauté dans la continuité. Après 40 ans de création, il demeure le plus brillant ambassadeur de la mode française dans le monde.

Paloma Picasso/Friend and Client

Yves gives women both extreme elegance and dash!

He put trousers into a woman's wardrobe and made our lives easier.

The clothes in his collections are always a series of elements, classic enough never to go out of style: you can put on a ten year old jacket and be perfect. He constructs clothes around the body, to hide or to reveal just enough: with him, you can be fat or thin and you will always turn out just right. He creates protective clothes, by day to look your best going to work, by night to be more extroverted, more seductive.

With each collection he creates an emotion, not only beautiful clothes.

Yves donne aux femmes une extrême élégance et du panache!

Il a mis le pantalon dans la panoplie féminine, et nous a rendu la vie plus facile.

Les vêtements de ses collections ont toujours assez d'éléments de classicisme pour ne pas passer de mode: on peut prendre une veste d'il y a dix ans et être parfaite. Il construit les vêtements autour du corps, pour cacher et montrer ce qu'il faut: avec lui, on peut être grosse ou maigre on est toujours très bien. Il crée des vêtements protecteurs, le jour pour être au meilleur de sa forme en allant au travail, le soir pour être plus extravertie, plus séductrice. A chaque collection, il crée une émotion, pas seulement de beaux vêtements.

Helmut Newton/Photographer

Yves Saint Laurent has inspired my best fashion photos: the "smoking" rue Aubriot in Paris; the man on his knees rolling down the stocking of a woman in a tailored suit at the Trocadero; a color photo for French Vogue of all the mannequins in the couture salon; a series of couples in tailored suits kissing each other... I like the ambiguous side of his fashion for the "grande bourgeoisie". There are so few people with whom I feel completely in accord. And he, he is so touching, so fragile.

Yves Saint Laurent m'a inspiré mes plus belles photos de mode: le smoking pris la nuit, rue Aubriot dans Paris; l'homme à genou, qui déroule le bas d'une femme en tailleur, au Trocadéro; une photo en couleurs pour Vogue France, tous les mannequins dans le salon de la maison de couture; une série de couples en tailleur qui s'embrassent.

J'aime l'ambiguité de sa mode pour la grande bourgeoisie. Il y a si peu de gens avec qui je suis complètement d'accord. Et lui, il est émouvant, si fragile.

Nick Knight/Photographer

To me, Yves Saint Laurent is the essence of elegance, a sure value, a reference. As a child when we lived in Paris and I saw my mother dressed to go out, she wore Saint Laurent. It was the picture of gaiety and style.

Pour moi, Yves Saint Laurent est un basique de l'élégance, une donnée stable, une référence. Enfant, quand nous habitions Paris et que je voyais ma mère prête à sortir, elle portait du Saint Laurent. C'était l'image de la gaieté et du raffinement.

Clara Saint/Press Director,"Yves Saint Laurent Rive Gauche"

It was in 1962 or 1963 that I met the two of them, Pierre Bergé and Yves Saint Laurent, at a luncheon with Margot Fonteyn. We have hardly ever been apart since.

When Yves decided to create Rive Gauche, he wanted a small out-of-the-way boutique. He chose the rue de Tournon where there were only book shops and dealers in engravings. He asked me to take care of the press service because I wasn't working and it seemed such a small thing.

It was the first boutique opened by a great couturier outside the walls of the fashion house. It was young, subversive, and, considering the chosen part of town, had an "intellectual" connotation.

To me, Yves is neither a costume designer nor a couturier. He is an artist whose chosen field is clothing. He is on par with Andy Warhol, with so many others. He decided on "his" fashion very early on and I don't think he changes, ever. He has invented clothes once and for all for the woman's wardrobe which he has completely transformed. He formulated the basics of today's panoply.

There are lots of girls who dress in other boutiques - but they are dressed in the style he created, in the kind of clothes he created for everyday life in all countries.

C'était en 1962. Je les aie rencontrés tous les deux, Pierre Bergé et Yves Saint Laurent à un déjeuner avec Margot Fonteyn. Depuis, on ne s'est pas vraiment quittés.

Quand Yves a décidé de faire "Rive Gauche", il voulait une toute petite boutique, excentrée. Il a choisi la rue de Tournon, rien que des libraires et des marchands de gravures. Il m'a proposé de m'occuper du service de presse parce que je ne travaillais pas et que ça paraissait une toute petite chose... C'était la première boutique de grand couturier ouverte hors les murs de la maison de couture. C'était jeune, subversif, et, vu le quartier choisi, avec une connotation intello.

Pour moi. Yves ce n'est ni un designer ni un couturier. C'est un artiste, dont la discipline est le vêtement. Il est de plain pied avec Andy Warhol, avec bien d'autres. Dans sa mode, il s'est décidé très tôt et je ne crois pas qu'il change. Il a inventé des vêtements une fois pour toutes dans cette garde-robe féminine qu'il a transformée. Il a formulé les bases de la panoplie actuelle: il y a beaucoup de filles qui sont habillées ailleurs qu'ici mais elles portent le style qu'il a imposé, les ensembles qu'il a fait entrer dans la vie, dans la rue, dans tous les pays.

Paolo Roversi/Photographer

The perfect example of a great Parisian couturier is Yves Saint Laurent. The symbol. The myth. He is what brought me to Paris.

He has creativity, fantasy and imagination. He handles different themes with ease, with polish, with extravagance, with non-chalance. He is one of those rare designers who has never lost for one instant his sense of elegance. And elegance is a frame of mind based on timeless femininity whereas that which is "tuned-in" to the latest fashion burns itself out in one season.

L'image pour moi du grand couturier parisien c'est Yves Saint Laurent. Le symbole. Le mythe. Ce qui m'a amené à Paris.

Il a une créativité, une fantaisie, une imagination. Il aborde des thèmes trés différents avec aisance, avec raffinement, avec extravagance, avec nonchalance. Et l'élégance c'est tout un esprit qui se base sur une féminité intemporelle, alors que ce qui est branché se brûle en une saison.

Marc Jacobs/Designer

In the 70s I used to see lots of very smart affluent young people around 60th Street. They wore velvet trousers, frilly blouses and leather headbands. They were all in Saint Laurent.... and that is what made me want to be a designer.

Today it is the only house which has such an aura. Saint Laurent's fashion no longer provokes a shock of novelty but Yves Saint Laurent knows not only how to create but also how to maintain. Chanel and Vionnet preceded him on this path. It is extraordinary to be so sure of oneself, sure of one's evolution after having created a revolution.

Dans les années 70, je voyais une jeunesse dorée à New York sur la soixantième rue. Les filles portaient des pantalons de velours, des blouses à volants, des bandeaux de cuir sur le front. Elles étaient chic. Elles étaient en Saint Laurent. Et ça me donnaient envie de créer de la mode.

Aujourd'hui, c'est la seule maison qui ait une telle aura. La mode Saint Laurent, ce n'est plus le choc de la nouveauté, mais Yves Saint Laurent a su créer et a su maintenir. Chanel, Vionnet l'avaient précédé dans cette démarche. Mais c'est extra-ordinaire d'être aussi sur de soi, sur de son évolution après avoir créé la révolution…

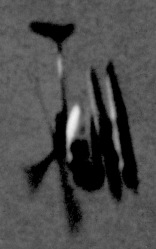

Jeanloup Sieff/Photographer

I am not a fashion photographer, but sometimes pleasure in my work has come from clothing. And these rare photographic pleasures have always been thanks to Yves Saint Laurent.

Je ne suis pas un photographe de mode, mais quelquefois dans mon travail, le plaisir est venu du vêtement. Et ces rares plaisirs photographiques sont toujours arrivés grâce à Yves Saint Laurent.

Lucie de la Falaise/Model

I was sixteen when I started to work at Saint Laurent and it was like a fairy tale for several hours-before getting back into my T-shirt and jeans!

It was wonderful to work in a great fashion house, with an authentic classic tradition. You know, when you are waiting for a fitting you are given a white smock to wear, but in other houses you just sit there shivering in your underwear...

And then to discover what it is all about: clothes made on you, which suit you...oh, the fittings!

But Yves, no, I don't know him well. We are both very shy and since he is shy it made me even shyer.

J'avais seize ans quand j'ai commencé à travailler chez Yves Saint Laurent, et c'était comme un conte de fées qui durait quelques heures-avant de se retrouver en T-shirt et en jean!

C'était merveilleux dans une grande maison, dans une tradition classique, très digne: vous savez, quand on attend pour les essayages, on met une blouse blanche. Dans les autres maisons, on reste là, à grelotter en petite culotte...

Et puis la découverte que c'était: des vêtements faits sur vous, qui vous vont exactement...ah, les essayages!

Mais lui, Yves, non, je ne le connais pas bien: nous sommes tous les deux très timides, et comme il l'est, moi je l'étais encore plus.

Steven Klein/Photographer

Yves Saint Laurent...in my photos I want to show the timeless quality of his clothes. Yves Saint Laurent...je voudrais remettre ses vêtements dans le temps absolu.

Fernando Sánchez/Designer

Yves is my brother, my elected family. We both entered the school of the Chambre Syndicale de la Couture in Paris the same year. We were placed at tables back to back. When we turned around, there was an instant bonding. We had the same tastes, we liked the same films, we shared a love of color, the attraction for the light of North Africa.

If Chanel brought casualness to fashion, Yves has completely reinvented a woman's wardrobe.

Cocteau used to say that one should pay great attention to the young who achieve their dreams. Yves has lived his fantasies. His house in Deauville is very Proustian, but his bedroom is Louis II of Bavaria, with one window giving onto the sea and another onto the forest. He has always been intrigued by the image of Louis II and that room in his castle in Bavaria.

Yves, c'est mon frère, ma famille élective. Nous sommes entrés ensemble à l'Ecole de la Chambre Syndicale de la Couture, à Paris. On était placés à des tables dos à dos. Quand on s'est retournés, on s'est reconnus. On avait les mêmes goûts des couleurs, cette attirance pour la lumière d'Afrique du Nord.

Si Chanel a apporté la désinvolture dans la mode, lui, Yves, il a refait la panoplie des femmes.

Cocteau disait qu'il faut faire très attention aux jeunes gens qui réalisent leurs rêves. Lui, il a vécu ses fantasmes. Dans sa maison de Deauville qui est très proustienne, sa chambre c'est Louis II de Bavière, avec une fenêtre sur la mer, une autre sur la forêt. Il a beaucoup flirté avec l'image de Louis II. Il s'est fait là un château en Bavière.

Jean-Paul Goude/Photographer/Film Maker

When I was seventeen, I too worked at Dior-in the "pattern making department"- where I had taken a student's summer job. Oddly enough, it was Saint Laurent's exceptional talent as an illustrator, through which I recognized my very own heroes-Christian Bérard, Gruau, Tom Keogh-that I learned to appreciate his fashion.

Today, as opposed to some designers who don't seem to see the difference between the art world and the fashion industry, and who forget that a garment should enhance the individual who wears it, one can only admire Saint Laurent's humility. He has never stopped putting his tremendous talent at the service of women he dresses.

Quand j'avais dix-sept ans, moi aussi j'étais chez Dior-au département "Patronage"-où j'avais pris un job d'étudiant pour l'été. Curieusement, c'est à travers l'exceptionnel talent d'illustrateur de Saint Laurent, dans lequel je voyais poindre l'influence de mes propres héros-Christian Bérard, Gruau, Tom Keogh-que j'ai découvert sa mode.

Aujourd'hui, contrairement à certains créateurs qui confondent l'art contemporain avec la mode et semblent oublier qu'un vêtement se doit de mettre en valeur l'individu qui le porte, on ne peut qu'admirer l'humilité de Saint Laurent qui n'a jamais cessé de mettre son immense talent au service des femmes qu'il habille.

Koji Tatsuno/Designer

As soon as I began to be interested in fashion I discovered Yves Saint Laurent.

He has always been a master: avant-garde in his approach and therefore creating his own classics. When one starts with an avant-garde idea and gives it continuity, one makes a classic of it.

He has said that he would have liked to have invented jeans: that is the modern attitude he established in relation to ready-to-wear. The type of androgynous beauty he showed is that which inspires us today. It is thanks to him that women began to dress in a more contemporary way.

The image of Saint Laurent is the image of French style.

Aussitôt que j'ai commencé à m'intéresser à la mode, j'ai pris conscience de l'image Saint Laurent.

Il a toujours été un maître: avant-garde dans son attitude et par conséquent créant ses propres classiques. Quand on part d'une création d'avant-garde et qu'on lui donne une continuité, on en fait un classique.

Il a dit qu'il aurait voulu inventer les jeans: c'est cela l'attitude moderne qu'il a instauré vis a vis du prêt à porter. Le type de beauté androgyne qu'il a montré est celui qui nous inspire tous aujourd'hui. C'est grâce à lui que les femmes ont commencé à s'habiller de façon plus contemporaine.

L'image de Saint Laurent, c'est le style français.

Lamine Kouyate-Xuly Bet/Designer

Forty years already! Yves Saint Laurent-he is the one who has expressed a vision of the black woman which is positive, and rather lyrical. It is he who began to break down the walls of the way in which the Occident saw black beauty. He knew how to weave suspension bridges between different cultures.

When I began to design I found that my approach resembled his, perhaps unconsciously: the search for aesthetic moderation, not excess.

Quarante ans déjà! Yves Saint Laurent, c'est lui qui a apporté une image positive et assez lyrique de la femme noire. C'est lui qui a commencé à abattre les murailles de l'Occident vis à vis de la beauté noire. Il a su tisser des ponts entre des cultures différentes.

Quand j'ai commencé à travailler, j'ai trouvé que ma démarche se rapprochait peut-être inconsciemment de la sienne: la recherche de l'esthétique dans la sobriété.

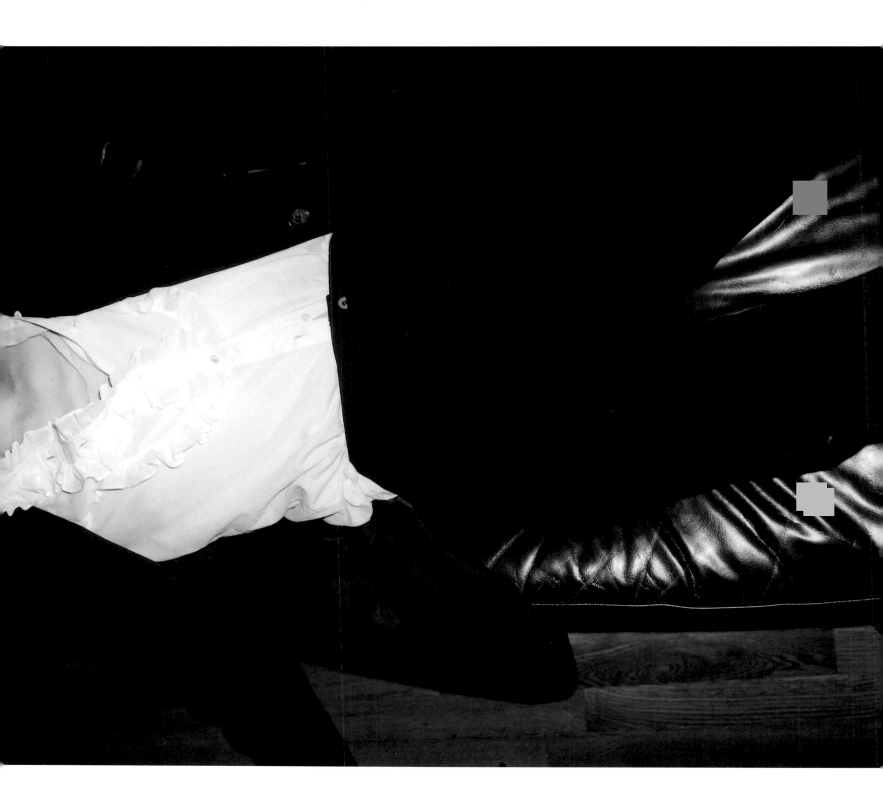

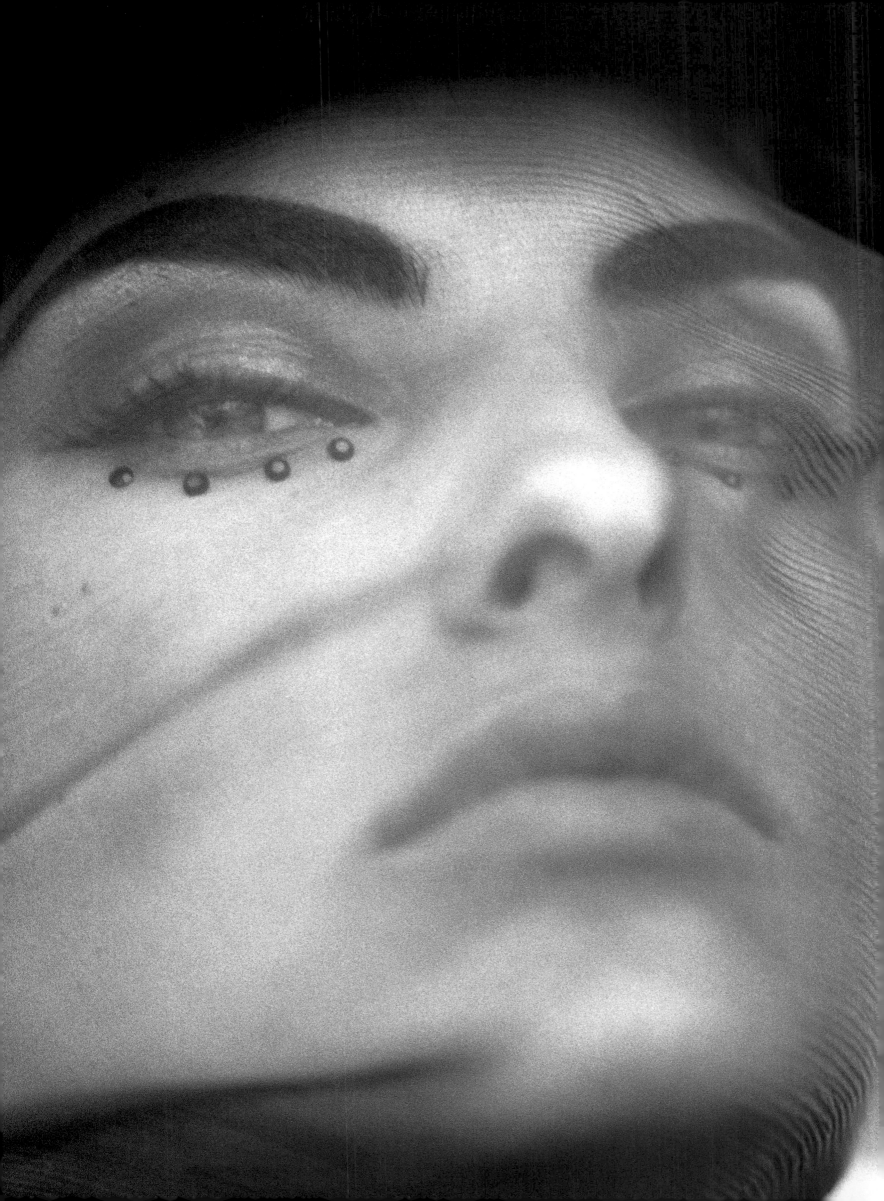

Terry/Creative Cosmetics Director/Yves Saint Laurent Parfums

I need to work for a brand name which is inspired by a creator, not just a trademark. A brand name which owes its life to a creator masters its own identity. It is he who is the yardstick, against which everything must be measured. The range of color is always inspired by what I see at the fashion house during the fittings. But it is not only the fabrics themselves: one must add the imaginary, tell a story, translate but not copy. Create a language of color through cosmetics.

He is not much seen, but he sees everything, he is ever present. I don't want anyone to say it is I who creates: it is he, because it all stems from his fashion. For the fashion shows we try out different shades on the models for the skin, for the mouth. Some seasons he makes sketches. It was he who drew the first bi-colored lips. Yves Saint Laurent surpasses mere logic. It is this leap which creates the difference. And it is unique.

Everyone thinks that Pierre Bergé is the boss, they don't see that the real boss is Yves Saint Laurent. If he says, "I don't like it," it's dead. Pierre Bergé is fascinating because he never tries to influence him. He has guided him, protected him, supported him, mothered him, but never influenced him. What the artist wants, will be.

Pour travailler, j'ai besoin d'une marque animée par un créateur, pas désincarnée. Les marques qui vivent de leur créateur ont la maîtrise de leur identité.

Les gammes de couleurs sont toujours inspirées de ce que je vois à la maison de couture pendant les essayages. Mais ce ne sont pas seulement les tissus eux-mêmes: il faut y mettre de l'imaginaire, raconter une histoire, traduire, pas copier. Créer un langage couleurs en cosmétique.

On le voit très peu, mais il voit tout. Il est archi-présent. Je ne veux pas qu'on dise que c'est moi qui crée: c'est lui, parce que toute la création se rapporte à sa mode. Pour les collections, on fait des essais de carnation, de bouche, sur le mannequin. Il y a des saisons où il fait des croquis. C'est lui qui a dessiné les premières lèvres bicolores. Yves Saint Laurent, c'est la rupture avec la logique. C'est cet accident qui créé le décalage. Et c'est unique!

On croit toujours que Pierre Bergé est le patron, on ne voit pas que le vrai patron c'est Yves Saint Laurent. S'il dit "je n'aime pas," c'est terminé. Pierre Bergé est fascinant parce qu'il n'essaie jamais de l'influencer. Il l'a encadré, protégé, sublimé, materné, mais jamais influencé. Si l'artiste veut, ce sera.

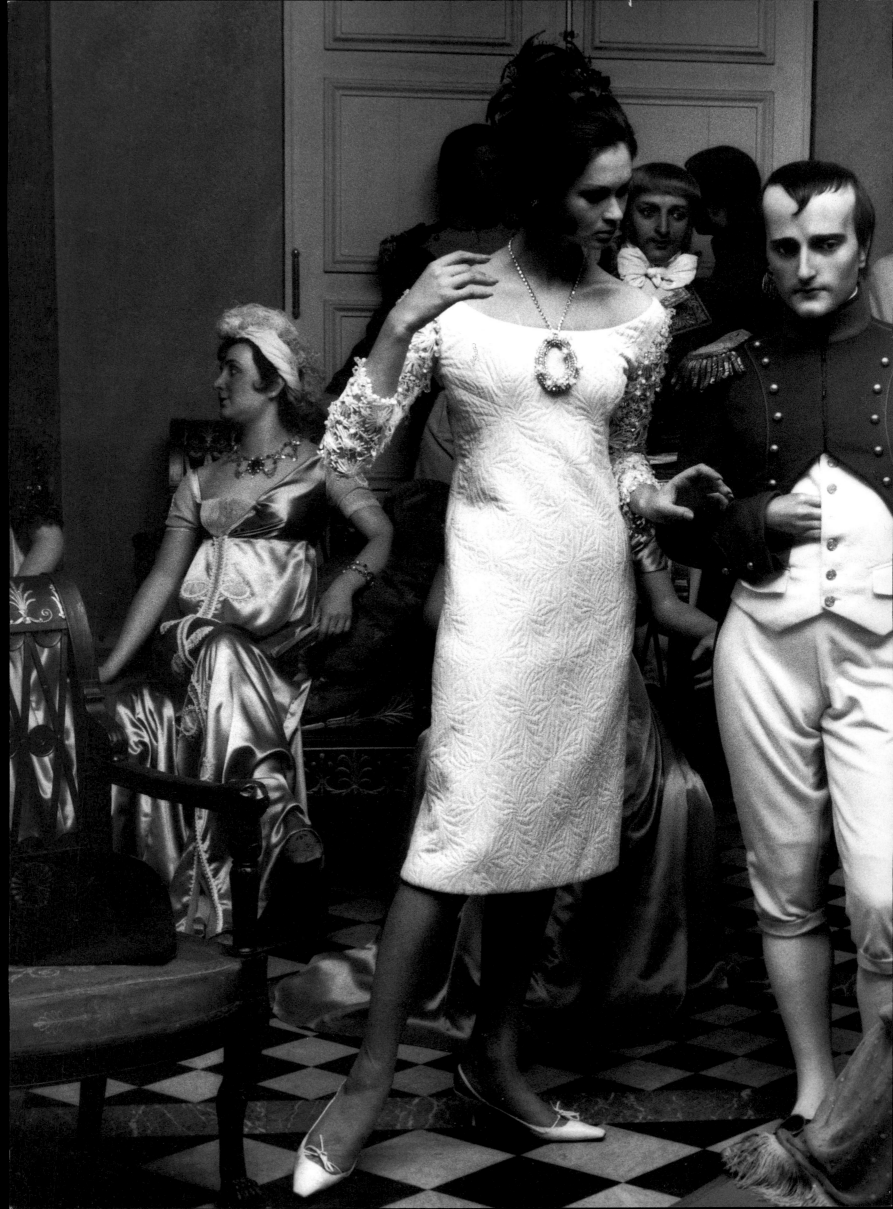

Christian Lacroix/Designer

I have often spoken of the shock I felt as a child (I was six years old) at the sight of the Paris Match cover showing Yves Saint Laurent between the short wedding dress from his first Dior collection and a bright red sack-coat. It was quite simply a shock of modernity, evident to a child, because it epitomized the age, the world to come, and was even a little ahead of its time since it was the first of March 1958 and heralded the birth of the sixties.

This was not an Yves Saint Laurent revolution, for what he was proposing had the "obviousness of a chef d'oeuvre," about which I believe Baudelaire speaks. Above all, it expressed perfectly the feeling of momentum between the usual convention, bourgeois elegance, which he quite naturally rendered obsolete, and the avant-garde, too anxious to be different at any price to be truly new. Saint Laurent's hour had come, neither too soon nor too late. Exactitude is the courtesy of kings - in fashion too.

Yves Saint Laurent seems to me the "enfant terrible", descended of course from Dior but above all from Chanel, Schiaparelli, and Balenciaga, the heir of the world of Bérard, Cocteau and Picasso, with the obligation and the talent to enrich this inheritance.

The rigor of Vélasquez as interpreted by Balenciaga becomes the delicacy of Goya with Saint Laurent. The Chanel "uniform" is perpetuated by a modern army wearing a khaki bushjacket. As for Schiaparelli's surrealism, he has assimilated it so well that were she alive today she would still be wearing Saint Laurent as she did until the end of her life.

How could it be possible not to be influenced by this coexistence which represents the century, not to mention the orientalism to which each era succumbed?

After so many tributes and so many images, forty years later Yves Saint Laurent seems to want to focus on essentials, still rebelling against stultifying convention (forever a threat) still with the same zest for "elsewhere" whether by means of a journey or through his readings.

Everything has been said about Yves Saint Laurent - even a little of the truth. Like Cocteau, whom to me he resembles in many ways, he possesses the essential power to astonish over and over again.

I remember especially shoulders, wide trousers, polka dot or lace dresses cleverly crafted, 1940s boaster worn straight, shading the eyes, it is, in fact, the stunning image of Madame Saint Laurent which her son serenaded, glorified and imposed all through this almost half-century. I only met her once and I expressed this interpretation to her with a certain shyness. She replied that in fact we shared a secret: the secret of the South, of the Mediterranean, and of the power of its sky over colors.

J'ai souvent évoqué le choc véritable que j'avais ressenti, enfant (j'avais six ans), devant la couverture de Paris Match montrant Yves Saint Laurent entre la mariée courte de sa première collection Dior et un manteau-sac rouge. C'était tout simplement un choc de modernité, palpable par un enfant car il traduisait l'époque, un monde naissant avec même un peu d'avance puisque c'était le 1er Mars 1958 et que c'était déjà le faire-part de naissance des années 60. Il n'y a pas eu de révolution Yves Saint Laurent car ce qu' il proposait avait l'évidence "chefs d'oeuvre" dont parle Beaudelaire je crois, avec, surtout, le sens du "momentum", si juste, entre l'élégance convenue, bourgeoise et conventionnelle en cours, qu'il rendit tout naturellement obsolète et les avant-gardismes trop "nouveaux a tout prix" pour être vraiment neufs. Son heure était venue ni trop tôt, ni trop tard. C'est une exactitude qui est la marque des rois, en mode aussi.

Bien sur il y avait non seulement Dior, mais surtout Chanel, Schiaparelli et Balenciaga dont Yves Saint Laurent me semble l'enfant terrible, héritier d'un monde, celui de Bérard, Cocteau et Picasso, avec le devoir et le talent de faire fructifier cet héritage.

La rigueur "Velasquiene" de Balenciaga a trouvé avec lui les délicatesses de Goya. L'uniforme de Chanel est perpétué jus qu'à devenir la saharienne kaki d'une armée moderne. Quant au surréalisme de Schiaparelli, il l'avait si bien intègré qu'elle s'habillerait encore avenue Marceau aujourd'hui comme elle le fit jusqu'à la fin de sa vie si elle était encore de ce monde.

Comment ne pas être influencé par ce syncrétisme de tout un siècle, sans oublier l'orientalisme auquel toutes les époques auront cédé.

Après tant d'hommages et d'images, Yves Saint Laurent, quarante ans après, semble vouloir atteindre l'essentiel, toujours rebelle a la bourgeoisie sclérosante qui pourtant menace souvent de le rattraper, toujours avide d'"ailleurs", que ce soit l'espace du voyage ou le temps de la lecture.

On a tout dit sur Yves Saint Laurent et même un peu de vrai. Et de Cocteau, dont il me semble partager tant de traits, il garde le vital pouvoir du perpétuel étonnement.

Ce que moi je garde surtout en mémoire: des épaules, un pantalon large ou des robes savantes à pois, à fleurs ou en dentelle, canotiers 40 sur l'oeil: c'est en fait l'image miraculeuse de Madame Saint Laurent mère que son fils aura propagée, chantée et imposée tout au long de ce presque demi-siécle. Je ne l'ai rencontrée qu'une fois et j'ai tenu a lui rendre cet hommage timide. Elle m'a répondu que nous partagions en fait un secret: celui du Sud, de la Méditerranée et du pouvoir que son ciel a sur les couleurs.

Yves Saint Laurent a codifié le vêtement féminin de la seconde moitié du vingtième siècle.

Il a créé le tailleur moderne: une belle carrosserie, comme un avion parfait. C'est la veste qui a accompagné la montée du féminisme, le vêtement de protection pour cacher les attributs féminins pour la femme dans le milieu du travail, mais il y a toujours cette encolure qui dégage la minceur du cou, ces manches qui dégagent la fragilité des poignets, cette taille menue qui contraste avec les épaules larges.

Il a inventé et perfectionné les proportions harmoniques.

Aujourd'hui, dans la mode, tout se passe dans son ombre, ou en opposition à lui.

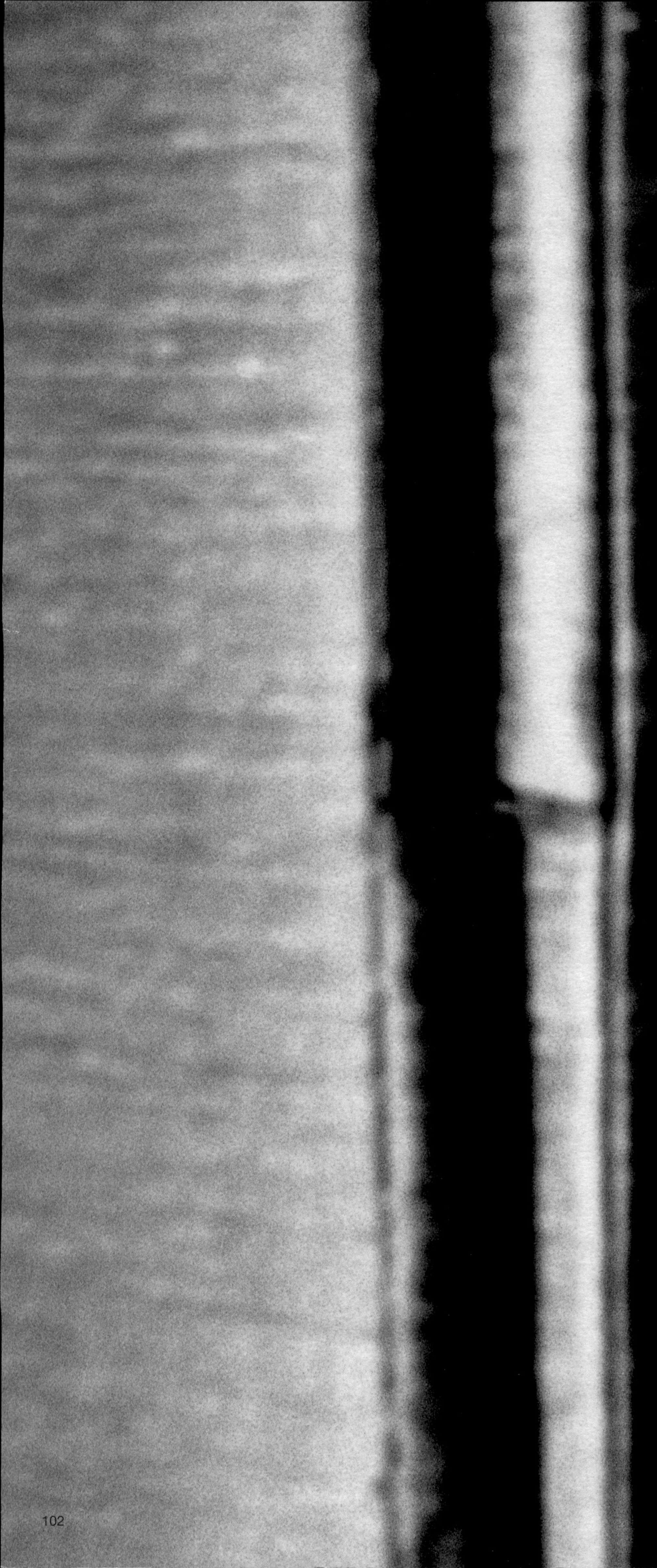

Maïmé Arnodin/"Nomad" Agency, Paris

I met Yves Saint Laurent when my company was engaged to work on the launch of the perfume "Opium". We showed him everything. He would say, "Perhaps one could…". He was always right.

For the press kit for "Kouros", he brought piles of sketches and said, "Choose…", he also wrote the texts. For "YSL", when we showed him Sacha's photos on the lightbox, the photos of flowers in the water and in the desert, he had tears in his eyes.

From the very beginning he has brought everything to fashion, all the great classics, and with elegance and ease. Those who design clothes today rework these famous classics, his small squared shoulder, his fantasy, his ethnic influence, his transparencies.

He is an artist, not a couturier. And that is the difference.

Yves Saint Laurent je l'ai rencontré pour le lancement du parfum "Opium" auquel nous avons travaillé. On lui montrait tout. Il disait: "Peut-être qu'on pourrait…". Il avait toujours raison.

Pour le dossier de presse de "Kouros", il arrivait avec des piles de croquis, il disait: " Choisissez…" il écrivait aussi les textes. Pour "YSL", quand on lui a montré sur la table de visionnage les photos de Sacha, ces fleurs dans l'eau et dans le désert, il a eu les larmes aux yeux…

Depuis qu'il a commencé, il a tout apporté dans la mode, tous les grands classiques, avec élégance et avec confort. Ceux qui font de la mode aujourd'hui reprennent ces fameux classiques, sa petite épaule carrée, et sa fantaisie, le côté ethnique, les transparences.

C'est un artiste, pas un couturier. C'est ça la différence.

Betty Catroux/Friend and client

We met in 1966-he picked me up in a night-club. We both had long pale blond hair, were both very thin, and were both dressed in black leather. Perhaps that is why. Ever since then he has been my best friend. We are sensitive to the same things and tremendously at ease with each other, as if we were blood relations.

When he goes to Marrakech I always go to spend a few days with him. We swim in the pool, he is very relaxed. Paris is the mirror of anxieties, Marrakech is the place where he is happy.

On s'est rencontrés en 1966, il m'a dragué dans une boite. On était blonds pâle tous les deux, les cheveux longs, maigres, habillés pareil en cuir noir. C'est peut-être pour cela. Mais depuis, il est mon meilleur ami. On a la même sensibilité, on est follement à l'aise ensemble: comme si on était du même sang.

Quand il va à Marrakech je vais toujours passer quelques jours avec lui. Nous nageons dans la piscine, il est très détendu. Paris, c'est le miroir de ce qui l'angoisse. Marrakech, c'est le lieu du bonheur.

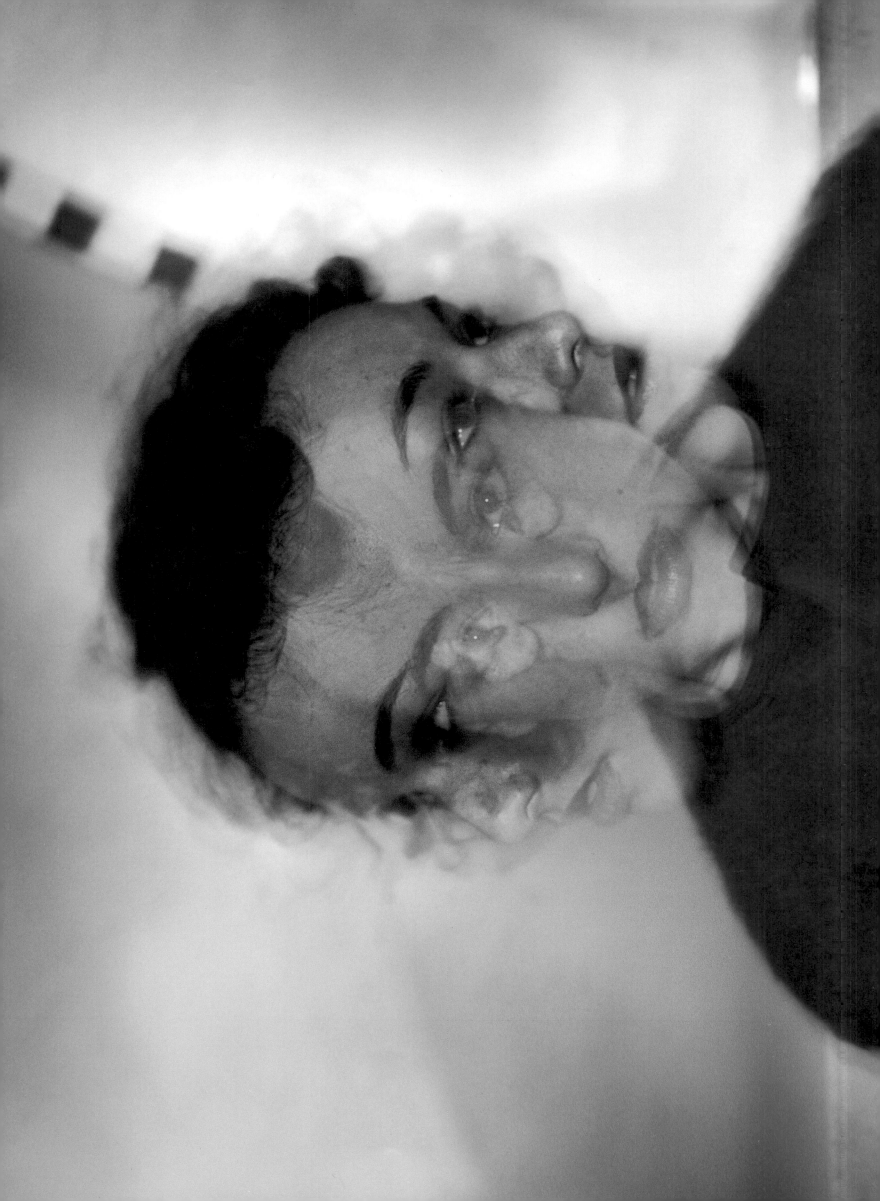

Jerome Faillant Dumas/Art Director, Yves Saint Laurent.

The photograph that touches me the most is the portrait Mr. Penn did for the exhibition at the Museum of Decorative Arts in Paris in 1986 because he exudes in his work intelligence and not only subjectivity. Mr. Penn knows how to pinpoint the essential: timidity - and the extremely piercing look that sees everything.

La photo qui me touche le plus c'est le portrait que Monsieur Penn a fait pour l'exposition de 1986 au Musée des Arts Décoratifs à Paris, parce qu'il apporte dans son travail une intelligence, et pas seulement une subjectivité. Monsieur Penn a su détecter l'essentiel: la timidité-et le regard-ce regard extrêmement perçant et qui voit tout.

Marian McEvoy/Editor in Chief, Elle Décor

Yves Saint Laurent.
A friend.
A rare talent.

His style is a mixture of charm and chic, of bittersweet, of strict and soft. Nothing is ever forced, but in his work one finds a certitude, a love of life, and always cultural references. His collections are a lesson in elegance: a woman can go out wearing the dress, the accessories, the coiffure and be just right.

His talent for decor is as great as his talent for fashion. His houses have influenced all contemporary interior decorators.

I have been formed by Saint Laurent's taste. It is a vision of beauty, of fashion, of women which is very discerning and very respectful.

Yves Saint Laurent.
Un ami.
Un talent très rare.

Son style est un mélange de charme et de chic, de doux-amer, de sec et de flou. Rien n'est jamais forcé, mais dans son travail on trouve une certitude et une joie de vivre, des références culturelles. Ses collections sont une leçon d'élégance: une femme peut sortir avec la robe, les accessoires, la coiffure, et être bien.

Son talent dans la mode se retrouve dans son sens du décor. Ses maisons ont influencé tous les décorateurs contemporains.

J'ai été formée par le goût d'Yves Saint Laurent. C'est une vision de la beauté, de la mode, des femmes, qui est très fine et très digne.

Anne-Marie Perier, Editorial Director, Elle France

I was not born with an interest in fashion, but when I began to work and to buy my own clothes, I only bought Saint Laurent ready to wear. He gave me a lesson in style, in allure.

He has always been faithful to what he likes and rigorous in the interpretations he gives to his sources of inspiration, and often moving.

He is quite apart and his style is eternal.

His importance today? Look at the importance the fashion editors of Elle give him in the magazine!

Je ne suis pas née en m'intéressant à la mode, mais quand j'ai commencé à travailler-et à acheter moi-même mes vêtements - je n'ai choisi que du prêt à porter de Saint Laurent. C'est lui qui m'a donné le goût du vêtement, une leçon de style et d'allure.

Il témoigne d'une fidélité à ce qu'il aime, et d'une rigueur dans les interprétations qu'il fait de ses sources d'inspirations, vraiment émouvantes. Il est tout à fait à part, et son style est éternel.

Son importance aujourd'hui? Regardez l'importance que les rédactrices de mode de Elle donnent à Saint Laurent dans le magazine!

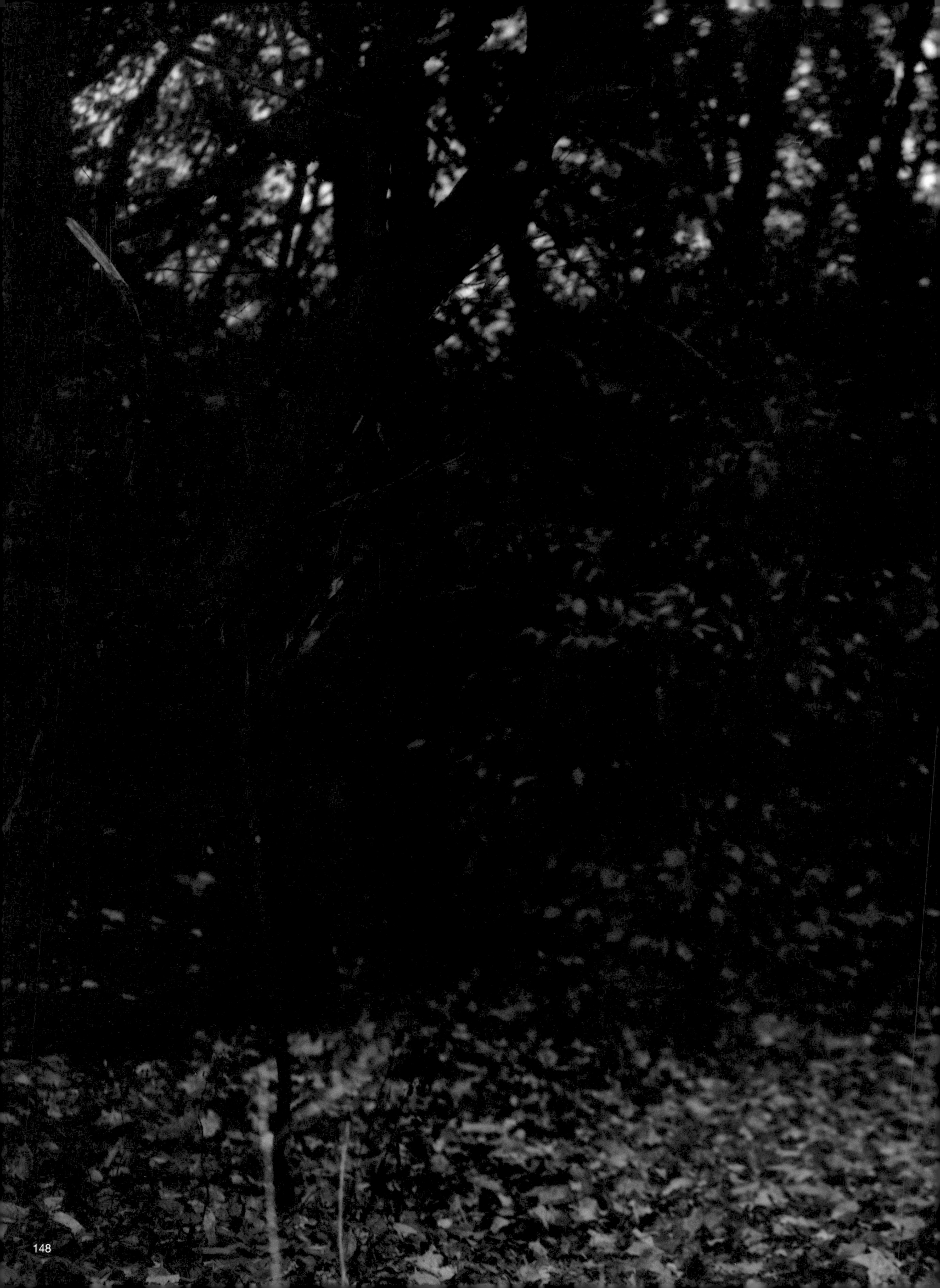

Mr. Yves
Saint
LaurEnt
in
tHe
sTudio

N Y Y C

Michel Klein/Designer

Yves Saint Laurent...he invented freedom. The possibility of erasing bourgeois dress codes while remaining luxurious. The play of color. Trousers in the city. Black legs. High heels with trousers. The freedom of lengths. He reinvented costume jewelry. Before the advent of Lycra he invented jersey jumpsuits.

The fact that he has a true Haute Couture image permitted him (like Chanel with jersey) to free all aspects of fashion.

Without harkening back to the past, without playing with disguise, he has created a contemporary fashion with very "cultural" inspirations. For Yves Saint Laurent, the influence of culture in all its aspects is only a source of inspiration.

Yves Saint Laurent... il a inventé la liberté. La possibilité d'effacer les codes de la bourgeoisie tout en faisant du luxe. Les jeux de couleur. Le pantalon en ville. Les jambes noires. Les talons hauts avec le pantalon. La liberté des longueurs. Il a réinventé le bijou fantaisie. Avant l'apparition du Lycra il a inventé les combinaisons de jersey.

Le fait qu'il ait une vraie image Haute Couture lui a permis (comme à Chanel avec le jersey) toutes les libertés dans la mode.

Sans être passéiste, sans jouer le déguisement, il a créé une mode contemporaine avec aussi des inspirations très "culture." Les influences pour Yves Saint Laurent sont plutôt des sources d'inspiration.

Paul Smith/Designer

The first "transparent effect" was designed by Yves Saint Laurent in 1971. A single layer of chiffon for a blouse worn under a tailored jacket which you could take off or not. Today the transparencies shown from the beginning to the end of a collection seem to me, on the contrary, of so little necessity. Who is going to go out like that?

It was he who showed the first red fox coat-also the first "smoking"-adventurous-confident of its place in a woman's wardrobe.

Yves Saint Laurent creates without ever compromising either on quality, cut, color, or in fabric. He has assured a continuity in his creation and in any sphere that is what is most difficult. The incredible respect people have for him is evident.

Le premier effet de transparence, c'était signé Yves Saint Laurent en 1971. Une blouse de mousseline portée sous un veston, donc montrée-si on le voulait bien. Aujourd'hui les transparences exhibées d'un bout à l'autre d'une collection me semblent au contraire si peu nécessaires. Qui va se promener comme ça?

Le premier manteau de renard rouge, c'est lui qui l'a montré et aussi le premier smoking-aventureux, positif dans le porter, dans la garde-robe des femmes.

Yves Saint Laurent a créé sans jamais accepter de compromis sur la qualité, la coupe, la couleur, le tissu. Il a assuré une continuité à sa création, et dans tous les domaines c'est ce qu'il y a de plus difficile. Mais vous voyez l'incroyable respect que tout le monde a pour lui.

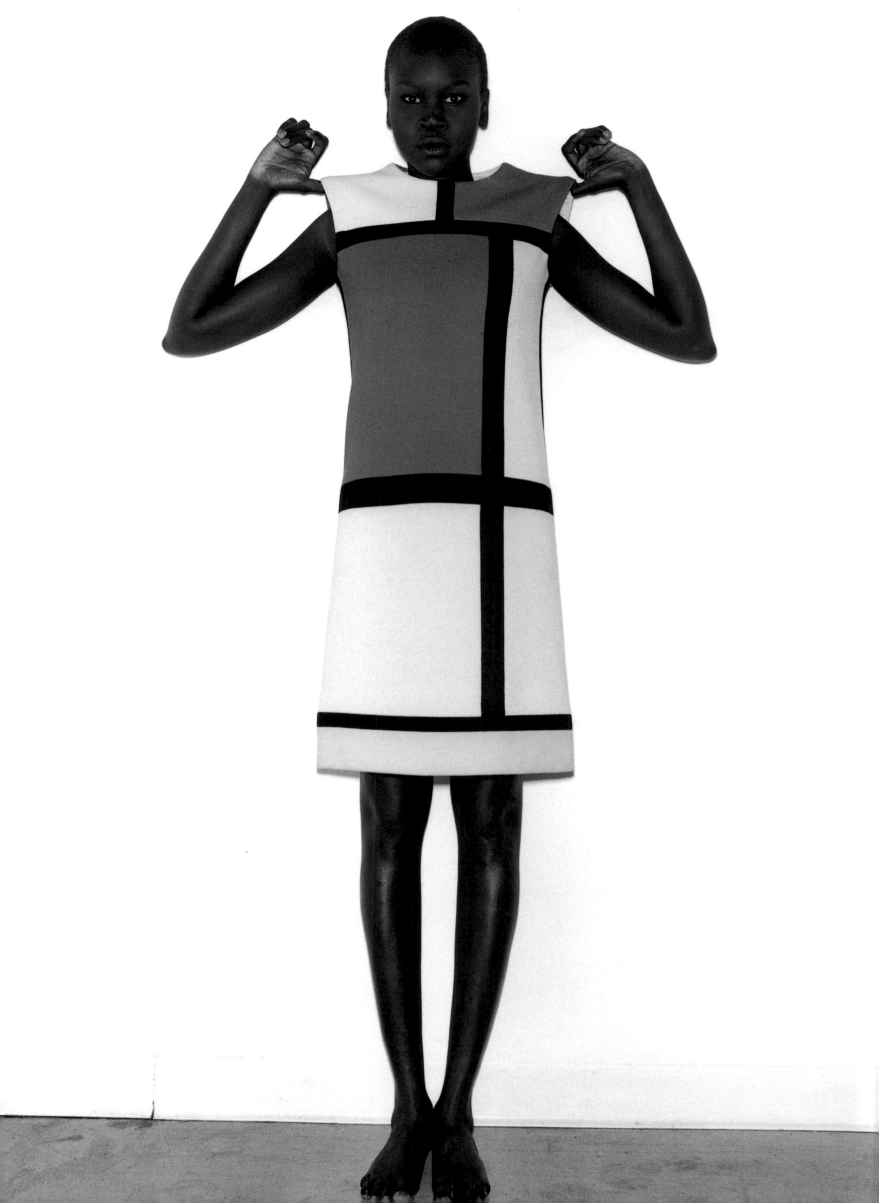

Suzy Menkes/Fashion Journalist, International Herald Tribune

Yves Saint Laurent is the most important fashion creator, couturier, of the second half of this century. So far ahead!

Before anyone else he understood the androgene, that women are like men, they want to work, they want to be recognized. Thirty years after he showed it on the runway women are still wearing pantsuits, blazers, trousers. Today it seems normal, everyday, but then it was scandalous; hotels, restaurants, refused to let you in...The "smoking" photo by Helmut Newton was pure sexual provocation, the woman who wanted to play the other role.

At the same time Yves Saint Laurent understood that women also want to seduce gently. His collections are not simply masculine or feminine but are also about the feeling of silk against the body, floating, never tight. The whole secret is in the cut: strict or fluid, like wisps of fog caressing the body. Imagination, poetry, exquisite colors: his evening dresses continue to amaze us.

Yves Saint Laurent est le créateur de mode, le grand couturier le plus important de la deuxième partie du siècle. Tellement en tête!

Avant tout le monde il a compris l'androgynie, l'idée que les femmes sont comme les hommes, veulent travailler, veulent se voir reconnues. Trente ans après qu'il l'ait montré sur le podium, les femmes sont toujours en veston, en blazer un peu épaulé, en pantalon... Aujourd'hui cela parait normal, quotidien... à l'époque c'était scandaleux, on vous refusait l'entrée d'un hôtel, d'un restaurant... Le smoking, la photo de Helmut Newton, c'était une provocation sexuelle, la femme qui veut jouer l'autre rôle.

En même temps, Yves Saint Laurent a compris que les femmes veulent aussi séduire en douceur. Ses collections ne sont pas simplement le masculin au féminin, mais aussi la soie sur le corps, flottant, jamais serrée.

Tout le secret vient de la coupe: stricte ou fluide, comme des écharpes de brume qui descendent sur le corps. Imagination, poésie, couleurs exquises: le noir continue de nous étonner.

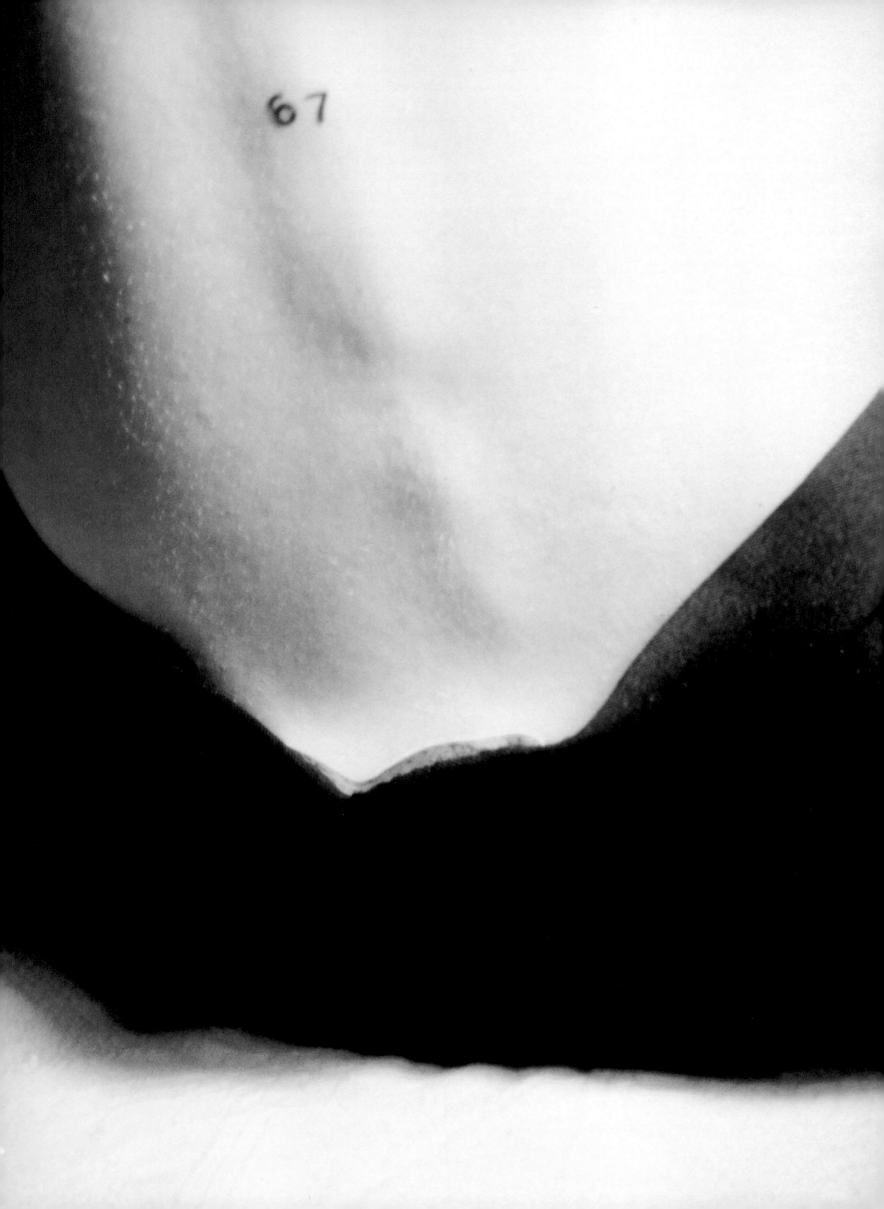

Bernadine Morris/Journalist

I was first aware of Saint Laurent's designs with his Trapeze dress around 1960. I wore it when I was pregnant. Later, things that appealed to me were the pea jacket and most significantly pants. In 1968 he showed an all-pants collection in Paris. It was the time of the student uprisings there as well as in this country. That single collection made it safe to wear pants. We are still doing it. That was perhaps his biggest contribution to the late-20th century dress. Also significant: was his emphasis on casual clothes as opposed to the rigors of the traditional haute couture. Long before I went to Paris to cover the collections (that was in 1970), I was familiar with his work through the line-for-line copies carried by Ohrbach's, the New York store. That's where I wore my trapeze and innumerable pant suits, including my favorite evening clothes, the dinner suit. He tended to show on the last day of the week and did so with such authority that all the other trends of the season fell into place.

His most impressive collection was the one called "haute Russian" in 1976. Everything was luxurious, extravagant and sumptuous. The significance was that after many years of pallid fashion, extravagance was back in style. It influenced designers around the world. The New York Times put my review on page 1 and devoted an entire page to it inside the paper. (I didn't suggest that: the editors decided that it was so important they would pull out all the stops). It was a high spot of his career-and mine too.

Yves would mix an inordinate amount of colors in the same outfit and everything would look preordained. A scarf in one shade, a blouse in another, gloves to contrast, a different lining - the list was endless and everything worked together. As far as color goes, Yves has perfect pitch.

Once, in an interview, he told me that a woman need only three things to look well dressed: a sweater, a pair of pants and a raincoat. There are worse definitions of fashion. What his statement indicates is that his feet are firmly on the ground and his head is grounded in reality.

Perhaps Saint Laurent will be the last couturier, honoring dressmaking skills, but not utilizing them in ways that are bizarre or barbaric. There is always a cleanness about his designs. He never distorts the body. His clothes look effortless and they never interfere with movement. There is an old joke on Seventh Avenue. A manufacturer is asked to make something different. "What do you want?" he answers, "Three sleeves?"

Designers today, especially in the couture, feel compelled to offer fashion equivalent of three sleeves. Saint Laurent never felt that kind of desperation. Beautiful clothes are enough of an excuse for being.

J'ai remarqué les créations d'Yves Saint Laurent pour la première fois autour de 1960, avec la robe trapèze. Je l'ai portée quand j'attendais un bébé. Plus tard, j'ai aimé le caban, et plus encore les pantalons. En 1968, c'était l'époque des émeutes d'étudiants à Paris comme aux Etats-Unis, il a montré une collection toute en pantalons. Cette collection suffit à officialiser le port du pantalon. Nous le portons toujours, et c'est probablement sa contribution la plus importante à la garde-robe de cette fin de siècle. Significative aussi, l'importance qu'il donne aux vêtements décontractés-par opposition à la rigueur de la Haute Couture traditionnelle. Longtemps avant qu'en 1970 j'ai commencé à venir à Paris pour "courir" les défiles de Haute Couture, je connaissais bien son travail grâce aux reproductions commercialisées par Ohrbach's, le magasin new-yorkais. J'y ai acheté d'innombrables tailleurs-pantalons, y compris des smokings, mes ensembles favoris pour le soir.

Il montrait sa collection le dernier jour, et le défilé avait une telle autorité que toutes les tendances de la saison s'organisaient logiquement à partir de là.

Sa collection la plus spectaculaire a été celle baptisée "Grande Russie" en 1976. Luxueuse, extravagante, somptueuse. Après des années de mode incolore, c'était le retour de l'extravagance. Les créateurs du monde entier en ont été influencés. Le New York Times a publié mon compte-rendu en première page et y a ajouté une pleine page intérieure. Ce ne fut pas à ma demande: la rédaction en chef trouve l'énvénement si important qu'elle décide de bousculer les priorités habituelles. Ce jut un moment fort de la carrière d'Yves Saint Laurent-et aussi de la mienne!

Yves réunit une quantité immodérée de couleurs sur un même ensemble avec un air d'évidence: un foulard d'une couleur, la blouse d'une autre, les gants contrastants, une doublure différente, et tout fonctionne bien. Pour la couleur, Yves pratique l'accord parfait.

Il m'a dit un jour qu'une femme n'avait besoin que de trois choses pour être bien habillée: un pull, un pantalon et un imperméable. Il y a de pires définitions de la mode. Il voulait montrer par là son profond réalisme.

Il y a une vieille plaisanterie à New York, dans les milieux du prêt à porter. Un fabricant à qui on demande de faire quelque chose de différent répond, "Trois manches, par exemple?" Aujourd'hui, les créateurs, et particulièrement dans la couture, se sentent obligés de proposer "trois manches." Saint Laurent n'a jamais éprouvé ce besoin désespéré. La beauté lui semble, pour un vêtement, une raison suffisante d'exister.

Jean Colonna/Designer

Yves Saint Laurent? I say Monsieur Yves Saint Laurent, just as I say Mademoiselle Chanel.

Because he always endeavors to make a woman beautiful, and that forces respect. His culture, his memory, is part of his fashion. He has made it modern through masculine tailoring, bush jackets, variations on the dinner jacket and each time the costume is so right that there is nothing more to say. He does not cultivate the ornamental. No "couture" effects. He uses bias when it is necessary, otherwise he simply cuts on the straight. The fashion show is not a spectacle, and he is the only one to begin it with a big section of day clothes.

Monsieur Saint Laurent is discretion and perfection. What I admire about the man is that he suffers but it doesn't show in his work: the woman is victorious every time.

Yves Saint Laurent? Je dis Monsieur Saint Laurent, comme je dis aussi Mademoiselle Chanel.

Parce qu'il tend toujours à rendre une femme belle, et cela force le respect. Il a adapté à la mode sa culture, sa mémoire. Il a donné à cela une modernité avec les tenues masculines, les sahariennes, le smoking, et le modèle est à chaque fois tellement vrai qu'il n'y a rien à dire. Il ne cultive pas l'ornemental. Pas d'effets "couture." Il fait du biais s'il le faut, sinon c'est du droit fil dont on n'a pas honte. Le défilé n'est pas un show. C'est le seul qui commence par une grande séquence de vêtements de jour.

Monsieur Saint Laurent, c'est la discrétion et la perfection. Ce que j'admire chez cet homme c'est qu'il souffre et que ça ne se voit pas dans son travail: à chaque fois la femme en sort victorieuse.

10/11 Photographer: **Pierre Boulat**
Publication: *Life Magazine,* 1961
Agency: Cosmos

13-19 Photographer: **Steven Meisel**
Publication: *Vogue Italy*, March 1993
Hair: Garren
Make-up: Denise Markey
Stylist: Joe McKenna

21 Photographer: **Helmut Newton**
Publication: *Vogue Paris*, 1975

22/23 Photographer: **Nick Knight**
Publication: *Vogue Homme International*, Spring/Summer 1995
Model: Kwabeena
Stylist: Marc Ascoli

24/25 Photographer: **Terry Richardson**
for IFFP 1998
Outfit: robe de crepe de soir et dentelle noirs, Haute Couture Hiver 1970
Model: Nikki Uberti
Hair: Johnnie Sapong
Make-up: Francisco Valera
Stylist: Andrew Richardson

27 Photographer: **Jeanloup Sieff**
1971

29 Photographer: **Paolo Roversi**
Publication: *Vogue Italy*, September 1996
Model: Naomi Campbell
Hair: Julien d'Ys
Make-up: Pat McGrath
Stylist: Alice Gentilucci

30/31 Photographer: **William Klein**
1963

33 Photographer: **Mario Sorrenti**
Publication: *W Magazine*, October 1996
Model: Milla Jovovich
Hair: Drew Jarrett
Make-up: Kay Montano
Stylist: Alexandra White

34/35 Photographer: **Helmut Newton**
Publication: *Vogue Italy* December 1996
Stylist: Phyllis Posnick

36 Photographer: **Jeanloup Sieff**
1966

37 Photographer: **Jeanloup Sieff**
1970

38/39 Photographer: **Mark Borthwick**
for IFFP 1998
Dress: Blouse Normande 1962/1963
Model: Megan
Stylist: Desiree

40/41 Photographer: **Craig McDean**
Publication: *W Magazine*, April 1997
Model: Kate Moss
Hair: Julien d'Ys
Make-up: Pat McGrath
Stylist: Alexandra White

43 Photographer: **Juergen Teller**
Rive Gauche Campaign 1997
Model: Kate Moss
Hair: Ward
Make-up: Myranda Joyce
Stylist: Venetia Scott
Agency: Wolkof & Arnodin

44/45 Photographer: **Steve Hiett**
Publication: *Vogue Paris*, January 1996
Hair: Carlos
Make-up: Topolino
Stylist: Isabelle Peyrut

47-49 Photographer: **Steven Klein**
Publication: *Dutch*, November 1997
Model: Alyssa, Jamie Rishar, Meredith Cosgrove
Hair: Jimmy Paul
Make-up: Mark Carasquillo
Stylist: Matthias Vriens
Art Direction: Lisa Stevens

51 Photographer: **Peter Lindbergh**
Publication: *Vogue Paris*, March 1991
Model: Gisele
Hair: Odile Gilbert
Make-up: Stephane Marais
Stylist: Babeth Djian

52 Photographer: **Helmut Newton**
Publication: *Vogue Paris*, 1981

53 Photographer: **Juergen Teller**
Rive Gauche Campaign 1997
Model: Kate Moss
Hair: Ward
Make-up: Myranda Joyce
Stylist: Venetia Scott
Agency: Wolkof & Arnodin

55 Photographer: **Franco Rubartelli**
Publication: *Vogue Paris*, 1968
Model: Veruschka

56/57 Photographer: **Paolo Roversi**
Publication: *Vogue Italy*, March 1997
Model: Tasha Tilberg
Hair: Julien d'Ys
Make-up: Pat McGrath
Stylist: Alice Gentilucci

58/59 Photographer: **Guy Bourdin**
Publication: *Vogue Paris*, 1979

60/61 Photographer: **Arthur Elgort**
Publication: *Vogue Britain*, 1971

62/63 Photographer: **Juergen Teller**
Publication: *Vogue Britain*, June 1995
Model: Claudia Schiffer
Stylist: Tiina Laakkonen

64 Photographer: **Javier Vallhonrat**
Publication: *Vogue Paris*, October 1992
Model: Linda Evangelista
Hair: Valentin
Make-up: Linda Cantello

66/67 Photographer: **Guy Bourdin**
Publication: *Vogue Paris*, 1971

69 Photographer: **Steen Sundland**
for IFFP 1998
Outfit: robe barbare longue de perles de bois, Haute Couture Eté 1967
Model: Kiara
Stylist: Helena Havana Laffitte

70 Photographer: **Sante d'Orazio**
for IFFP 1998
Outfit: robe longue de velours noir, Haute Couture Hiver 1997
Model: Frankie Rayder
Hair: Peter Buckle
Make-up: Kristopher Buckle
Stylists: Annett Monheim, Kim Canter

71 Photographer: **Sante d'Orazio**
for IFFP 1998
Outfit: robe longue de mousseline bleue de Claude Lalanne, Haute Couture 1969
Model: Frankie Rayder
Hair: Peter Buckle
Make-up: Kristopher Buckle
Stylists: Annett Monheim, Kim Canter

72 Photographer: **Guy Bourdin**
Publication: *Vogue Paris*, 1974

73 Photographer: **Guy Bourdin**
Publication: *Vogue Paris*, 1976

75 Photographer: **David Bailey**
Publication: *Vogue Italy*, 1971

76/77 Photographer: **Albert Watson**
Publication: *Vogue Italy*, March 1990
Model: Helena Christiansen
Hair: Kerry Warn
Stylist: Manuela Pavesi

78 Photographer: **Cindy Palmano**
Publication: *Sunday Times Magazine*

80/81 Photographer: **Alex Antich**
for IFFP 1998
Outfit: premier Smoking, Haute Couture Hiver 1966
Model: Annett Monheim
Stylist: Annett Monheim

83 Photographer: **Max Vadukul**
Publication: *Vogue Paris*, September 1989
Model: Linda Evangelista
Hair: Yannick d'Is
Make-up: Thierry Mauduit
Stylist: Nicoletta Santoro

84/85 Photographer: **Blaise Reutersward**
for IFFP 1998
Outfit: robe de satin et dentelle noirs, Haute Couture Eté 1996
Model: Kim Inglisky
Hair: Stephane Lancien
Make-up: Christine Corbel
Stylist: Claire Dupont

87 Photographer: **Helmut Newton**
Publication: *Vogue Paris*, 1979

89 Photographer: **Enrique Badulescu**
Publication: *Vogue Paris*, May 1995
Model: Ines Rivero
Hair: Sebastian Richard
Make-up: Paco Blancas
Stylist: Delphine Treanton

90/91 Photographer: **William Klein** 1963

92-95 Photographer: **Michel Haddi**
for IFFP 1998
Outfit: saharienne,
Haute Couture Eté 1968
Model: Veruschka
Hair: Damillo
Make-up: Mathu Anderson
Stylist: Terrence McFarland

98 Photographer: **Banu Cennetoglu**
for IFFP 1998
Outfit: robe de crepe de soie et
dentelle noirs, Haute Couture
Hiver 1970
Model: Ebony Ann Conway

99 Photographer: **Banu Cennetoglu**
for IFFP 1998
Outfit: cape et pantalon de Zouave,
Haute Couture Hiver 1979
Model: Ebony Ann Conway

101 Photographer: **Hans Feurer**
Publication: *Elle Paris*, 1971
Model: Willy Vanroy
Hair: Didier Malige
Make-up: Tyen
Stylist: Nicole Crassat

102/103 Photographer: **Pierre Boulat**
Agency: Cosmos
Publication: *Life Magazine*, 1961

105 Photographer: **Paolo Roversi**
Publication: *W Magazine*,
October 1997
Model: Stella Tennant
Hair: Julien d'Ys
Make-up: Mary Greenwell
Stylist: Michel Botbol

106/107 Photographer: **Laetitia Benat**
for IFFP 1998
Outfit: manteau "araignée",
Haute Couture Hiver 1970
Model: Anna R.

109 Photographer: **Bert Stern**
Publication: *Vogue*, 1967
Model: Twiggy

110 Photographer: **Michael Thompson**
Publication: *Vogue Paris*,
March 1997
Model: Shirley Mallman
Hair: Nicolas Jurnjack
Make-up: Frederic Farrugia
Stylist: Marcus Von Ackerman

113 Photographer: **Luis Sanchis**
for IFFP 1998
Outfit: cape et pantalon de Zouave,
Haute Couture Hiver 1979
Model: Rosalie Knox
Hair: Johnnie Sapong
Stylist: Gabriel Feliciano

114 Photographer: **Masha Calloway**
for IFFP 1998
Outfit: robe "cubiste",
Haute Couture Eté 1988
Model: Athena
Hair: Sariye
Make-up: Sariye
Stylist: John Hullum

115 Photographer: **Masha Calloway**
for IFFP 1998
Outfit: robe "panthère",
Hiver 1982
Model: Ruth
Hair: Sariye
Make-up: Sariye
Stylist: John Hullum

116/117 Photographer: **Helmut Newton**
Publication: *Vogue Paris*, 1981

118 Photographer: **Guy Bourdin**
Publication: *Vogue Paris*, 1965
Model: Jean Shrimpton

120/121 Photographer: **Christophe Cufos**
for IFFP 1998
Outfit: robe longue du soir de faille
et velours noirs, Haute Couture
Hiver 1993
Model: Violetta Sanchez
Hair: Terry Saxon
Make-up: Marie Madeleine Savin

122/123 Photographer: **Sandrine Expilly**
for IFFP 1998
Outfit: robe de mariée cocon,
Haute Couture 1965
Model: Nathalia
Make-up: Marie-Madeleine Savin
Assistant: Miguel

124/125 Photographer: **Max Vadukul**
Publication: *Vogue Paris*,
September 1989
Model: Linda Evangelista
Hair: Yannick d'Is
Make-up: Thierry Mauduit
Stylist: Nicoletta Santoro

126 Photographer: **Bettina Rheims**
YSL Backstage July 1981

128 Photographer: **Thierry Le Goues**
for IFFP 1998
Outfit: robe de plume d'oiseau de
Parade, Haute Couture Hiver 1969
Model: Li Xin
Hair: Stephanie Lancien
Make-up: Greshka

129 Photographer: **Thierry Le Goues**
for IFFP 1996
Outfit: Le Smoking

130/131 Photographer: **Terry Richardson**
for IFFP 1998
Outfit: robe de soir longue
de dentelle, Haute Couture
Hiver 1990
Model: Frankie Rayder
Hair: Dennis Lanni
Make-up: Nikki Uberti
Stylist: Andrew Richardson

133 Photographer: **William Klein**
Publication: *Vogue American*, 1962

134/135 Photographer: **Guy Bourdin**
Publication: *Vogue Paris*, 1976

136 Photographer: **Guy Bourdin**
Publication: *Vogue Paris*, 1971

137 Photographer: **Paolo Roversi**
Publication: *Vogue Britain*, May 1996
Model: Shalom
Hair: Julien d'Ys
Make-up: Pat McGrath
Stylist: Lucinda Chambers

138/139 Photographer: **Bettina Rheims**
YSL Backstage July 1981

140 Photographer: **Horst P. Horst**
Publication: *Vogue Paris*, 1979

141 Photographer: **Jean-Pierre Cade**
Courtesy Yves Saint Laurent Couture

142 Photographer: **Dietmar**
for IFFP 1998
Outfit: robe de plumes d'oiseau
de Parade, Haute Couture
Hiver 1969
Model: Amy Goodheart
Hair: Rolando Beauchamp
Make-up: Angie Parker
Stylist: Leila Minangi
Assistant: John Bumble

143 Photographer: **Jérome Albertini**
for IFFP 1998
Outfit: robe "Mondrian",
Haute Couture Hiver 1965
Model: Kristen Aka
Hair: Gio Campora
Make-up: Scott Patrick
Stylist: Annett Monheim
Assistant: Benji Strauss

144/145 Photographer: **Tiziano Magni**
for IFFP 1998
Outfit: Smoking, Haute Couture
Hiver 1994
Model: Ling
Hair: Bob Recine
Make-up: Yuki Wada
Stylist: John Hullum
Art Direction: Carlos Taylor

146 Photographer: **Andre Rau**
Publication: *Elle Paris*,
January 1992
Model: Catherine Deneuve
Hair: Charlie
Make-up: Thibault Vabre
Stylist: Frankie Mayer
Assistant: Christoph Sillem

147 Photographer: **Ellen Von Unwerth**
Publication: *Vogue USA*,
September 1991

148/149 Photographer: **Dietmar**
for IFFP 1998
Outfit: robe de jersey de laine,
Yves Saint Laurent Rive Gauche
Hiver 1996
Stylist: Sabina Kruz

150/151 Photographer: **Nigel Scott**
for IFFP 1998
Outfit: cape et pantalon de Zouave,
Haute Couture
Hiver 1979
Model: Jessy

152/153 Photographer: **Alexei Hay**
for IFFP 1998
Outfit: imperméable de ciré noir,
cagoule de cuir et cuissardes
crocodile, Haute Couture
Hiver 1963
Model: Mellisa Keller
Hair: Amanda
Make-up: Amanda
Stylist: Zita Tulvahikayo
Assistant: Rishad Mistpi

154 Photographer: **Michael Wooley**
Publication: *Elle Britain*,
February 1998
Model: Christelle
Hair: David Ralled
Make-up: Pascale Guichard
Stylist: Iain R. Webb

156 Photographer: **Laura Sciacovelli**
for IFFP 1998
Outfit: blouse de satin noir et
Smoking short, Haute Couture
Eté 1968
Model: Christelle Cervelle
Stylist: Jessica Doyle

157 Photographer: **Mikael Jansson**
Publication: *Vogue Paris*,
September 1996
Model: Mini Anden
Hair: Mike Lundgren
Make-up: Katerina Hakansson
Stylist: Delphine Treanton
Assistant: Priscilla Patron

159 Photographer: **Christoph Sillem**
for IFFP 1998
Outfit: robe "Mondrian",
Haute Couture
Hiver 1965
Model: Alec Wek
Hair: Nicolas Jurnjack
Make-up: Gwendoline

160 Photographer: **Faycal**
for IFFP 1998
Outfit: robe longue du soir,
Haute Couture 1993
Model: Anna R.
Hair: Sascha
Make-up: Sascha
Stylist: Corinne Moreau

161 Photographer: **Jan Welters**
for IFFP 1998
Outfit: robe de crepe de soir et
dentelle noirs, Haute Couture
Hiver 1970
Model: Jade Parfitt
Hair: Wataru
Make-up: Tracy Gray
Stylist: John Hullum

162 Photographer: **Bettina Rheims**
YSL Backstage July 1981

164 Photographer: **Christophe Jouany**
for IFFP 1998
Outfit: cape et pantalon de Zouave,
Haute Couture Hiver 1979
Model: Theresa Krenn
Hair: Thomas McGiver
Make-up: Theresa Pemberton

165 Photographer: **Kelly Klein**
Publication: *Harper's Bazaar*,
September 1997
Model: Shalom Harlow
Hair: James Brown
Make-up: Diane Kendal
Stylist: Tonne Goodman

166/167 Photographer: **Banu Cennetoglu**
for IFFP 1996
Outfit: premier Smoking,
Haute Couture Hiver 1966
Model: Carrie

169 Photographer: **Marcelo Krasilcic**
for IFFP 1998
Outfit: robe longue de mousseline
bleue de Claude Lalanne,
Haute Couture 1969
Model: Devra Kinery
Make-up: Devra Kinery

170/171 Photographer: **Lothar Schmid**
Publication: *Vogue Britain*, 1977

174 Photographer: **Jean Lariviere**
Publication: *Vogue Paris*,
October 1991
Hair: Ward
Make-up: Marc Schaelter

175 Photographer: **Bettina Komenda**
for IFFP 1998
Outfit: robe longue de velours noir,
Haute Couture 1997
Model: Nikky
Hair: Sebastian Richard
Make-up: Alice Ghendrih
Stylist: Claire Dupont

177 Photographer: **Miles Aldridge**
for IFFP 1998
Outfit: premier Smoking,
Haute Couture Hiver 1966
Model: Joanne W
Hair: Renato Campora
Make-up: Katarina Hakansson
Stylist: Annett Monheim

178/179 Photographer: **Jean-Claude Sauer**
1966

180 Photographer: **Michel Comte**
Publication: *Vogue Germany*,
June 1997
Model: Loulou de la Falaise

181 Photographer: **Jamil G.S.**
for IFFP 1998
Outfit: robe de plume d'oiseau
de Parade, Haute Couture
Hiver 1969
Model: Teresa
Hair: Frederic Parnell
Make-up: Carolina Gonzales
Stylist: Bernadette Van Huy
Artwork: Kaws

182/183 Photographer: **Gilles Bensimon**
Publication: *American Elle*,
January 1997
Model: Honor Fraser
Hair: Michel Aleman
Makeup: Fran Cooper
Stylist: Isabel Dupré

184 Photographer: **Walter Chin**
Publication: *Vogue Italy*,
July 1994
Model: Nina Brosch
Hair: Laurent Philippon
Make-up: Paul Starr
Stylist: Anna Dello Russo

185 Photographer: **Nina Schultz**
for IFFP 1998
Outfit: imperméable de ciré noir,
cagoule de cuir et cuissardes
crocodile, Haute Couture
Hiver 1963
Model: Dorota
Hair: Sariye
Make-up: Sariye
Stylist: Kim Carter

186/187 Photographer: **Ellen Von Unwerth**
Publication: *Vogue Paris*
Model: Catherine Deneuve
Hair: Charlie
Make-up: Régine Bedot
Stylist: Jenny Capitan
Assistant: Ralph Wenig

189 Photographer: **Platon**
Publication: *Harper's & Queen*,
April 1995
Model: Olga P.
Hair: James Dodds
Make-up: Jefferson
Stylist: Claire Todd

190 Photographer: **Francois Rotger**
for IFFP 1998
Outfit: robe longue du soir,
Haute Couture 1993
Model: Lyda
Hair: Giovanni Di Stefano
Make-up: Christine Corbel

191 Photographer: **Jeanloup Sieff**
1971-1972

193 Photographer: **Pierre Boulat**
Agency: Cosmo
Publication: *Life Magazine*, 1961

Acknowledgments-Yves Saint Laurent

Yves Saint Laurent
Pierre Bergé
Anne-Marie Munoz
Louise de la Falaise-Klossowski
Christophe Girard
Clara Saint
Ariel de Ravenel
Dominique Deroche
Hector Pascual
Eleonore de Musset
Myriam Rollin

Jerome Faillant-Dumas
Catherine Chevallier

Connie Uzzo
Don Loftus
Alison Mazzola

Agnes de Gouvion Saint Cyr,
Inspecteur Général pour la
Photographie, Ministère de la Culture.

Denise Dubois, Fédération Francaise
de la Couture, du Pret à Porter des
Couturiers et des Créateurs de Mode.

Stan Herman, President, Council
of Fashion Designers of America

Fern Mallis, Executive Director, Council
of Fashion Designers of America

The Fashion Institute of Technology

Texts and Translations
Marie-Jose Lepicard
Susan Train

Contributing Photographers
Jerome Albertini
Miles Aldridge
Alex Antich
David Bailey
Enrique Badulescu
Laetitia Benat
Gilles Bensimon
Mark Borthwick
Guy Bourdin
Pierre Boulat
Jean-Pierre Cade
Masha Calloway
Banu Cennetoglu
Walter Chin
Michel Comte
Christophe Cufos
Patrick Demarchelier
Dietmar
Sante d'Orazio
Arthur Elgort
Sandrine Expilly
Faycal
Hans Feurer
Michel Haddi
Alexei Hay
Steve Hiett
Horst P. Horst
Jamil G.S.
Mikael Jansson
Christophe Jouany

Kelly Klein
Steven Klein
William Klein
Nick Knight
Bettina Komenda
Marcelo Krasilcic
Jean Lariviere
Thierry Le Goues
Peter Lindbergh
Tiziano Magni
Craig McDean
Steven Meisel
Helmut Newton
Cindy Palmano
Platon
Andre Rau
Blaise Reutersward
Bettina Rheims
Terry Richardson
Francois Rotger
Paolo Roversi
Franco Rubartelli
Luis Sanchis
J.C. Sauer
Lothar Schmid
Nina Schultz
Laura Sciacovelli
Nigel Scott
Jeanloup Sieff
Christoph Sillem
Mario Sorrenti
Bert Stern
Steen Sundland
Juergen Teller
Michael Thompson
Max Vadukul
Javier Vallhonrat
Ellen Von Unwerth
Albert Watson
Jan Welters
Michael Wooley

Photographers Representatives
Abantu
Ado
Art & Commerce
Art Department
Art Partner, Giovani Testino
Katy Barker Agency
Marion de Beaupre
Blanpied/Rubini
Chris Boals
Cosmos
Isabelle Descamps
Michele Filomeno Inc., Michele Filomeno
& Rene Beaune
Marianne Houtenbras
Jean Gabriel Kauss
Thierry Kauffman
Lamprecht & Bennett
Therese Ryan Mahar
Noemie Mainguet
Marek & Associates
Catherine Mathis
Julian Meijer & Associates
Yannick Morisot
PMI/Photographic Management Inc.
Pamela Reid
Jed Root
Smile Management, Kim Sion
Streeters
Elizabeth Watson
Charlotte Wheeler
Wilson & Wenzel
Z Photographic, Ziggy Golding
& Katy Sabbag

Photographers Studios
Sante D'Orazio Studio, Joyce Mills
Arthur Elgort Studio, Michelle Ocampo
Nick Knight Studio, Emma Wheeler
Steven Meisel Studio, Julie-Anne Quay

Special Thanks
Marc Balet
Samuel Bourdin
Julie Brown
Joan Juliet Buck
Catherine Daydier
Patrick Demarchelier
Maher Dukar
Andre & Jeannette Dupire
Youmna & Ola Erstad
Sylvie Grumbach
Janah el Hassan
Richard Horst
Lloyd (+co) Alan Castro &
Maria Gustafson
Fadi Majdalani
Annett Monheim
Derek Penn
Jennifer Sage
Houda Ladki Sy
Cristina Trayfors
Veruschka

And all those personalities who
accepted to be interviewed.

Thank you to all the magazines
Dutch
Elle USA
Elle Paris
Harper's Bazaar
Harpers & Queen
I-D
LIFE
Sunday Times Magazine, London
Vogue American
Vogue Britian
Vogue Italy
Vouge Paris
Vogue Germany
Vogue Homme International
W

Thank you to all the model agencies
American Models
City Model Management
Company Management
DNA Model Management
Elite Model Management
FAM International
Ford Models
IMG Models
Irene Marie Agency-New York
Marilyn inc.
Model One
Nathalie
Next
Barbara Pfifter
Women Model Management

Labs
LTI, Scott Hagendorf
Lexington Labs, Laurent Girard
Picto Bastille, Pierre Guillemain
Picto Montparnasse, Laure Dagorn
Print Zone, Shazi
Sixty Eight Degrees

We would like to extend our thanks
to all the people without whom this
homage to Yves Saint Laurent, would
not have been possible.

Special thanks to all the photographers,
models, hair and make-up artists,
stylists, agencies and agents, studios
and assistants for their hard work and
kind support.

Team IFFP
Judy Elkan
Patrick Guillot
Bertha Katz
Tracey Mallalieu
Keisha Nicholas

Thanks to the City of New York.

Printed in the U.S.A. Bolger Printing, Minneapolis, MN

First edition 1998 ISBN 1-881616-98-3